He pelted her with profiteroles; she pinched his bottom under the table. Prince Andrew, returned from war a hero, and Sarah Ferguson, the exuberant redhead he had known in childhood, were both nursing bruised hearts when they met again as adults, but their jolly, rowdy romance was to culminate in the happiest of modern Royal marriages.

THOROUGHLY MODERN CHILDHOODS

PRINCE ANDREW WAS THE FIRST OF THE QUEEN'S 'SECOND FAMILY'; SARAH FERGUSON MIXED IN ROYAL CIRCLES THROUGH HER POLO-PLAYING FATHER: IT WAS INEVITABLE THAT THEIR PATHS SHOULD INTERTWINE EARLY IN THEIR LIVES

QUEEN ELIZABETH II HAD ALWAYS WANTED A large family and had fondly supposed that she would spend her child-rearing years on the royal sidelines as Heir Presumptive while her father continued to rule into old age. As it happened, his life was cut short at the age of 56 and she found herself Queen at 25 while her first two children were still tiny.

There was no question of having more children in that situation, and it was nearly ten years before she felt ready to cope with babies again. The long gap divided her children into what became spoken of as her 'first' and 'second' families. Andrew Albert Christian Edward, born on 19 February 1960, was the eldest of the second two children.

He was also the first of Elizabeth's children to bear the surname Mountbatten-Windsor — before this, her children had been known as Windsor only, with no reference to their father's name. This had bothered Prince Philip, who had once complained that it made him seem like a 'bloody amoeba'.

Close to mother

Andrew was a lovely, round, placid baby — 'a charmer', Princess Anne said later. His nurse remembered him as 'always full of smiles', and he was soon nicknamed 'Andy Pandy' by the Buckingham Palace staff.

Elizabeth was now well on top of her job, and had already decided that she would devote more time to this child than she had been able to do to his elder siblings. That didn't mean she neglected her work — indeed, she

♔ The proud mother with her new baby right. Andrew's names remained a secret for over a month – perhaps an indication of the Queen's determination to protect her son as much as possible from press and public attention

♔ A cheer went up from the crowds outside the Palace when the notice inset right announcing the Queen's safe delivery appeared. Andrew was born in the Belgian Suite, on the ground floor overlooking the gardens, and weighed 7lb 3oz

♔ Below Baby Prince Andrew smiles happily from his pram as he holds the hands of Princess Anne and the Duke of Edinburgh in the gardens of Balmoral. The little Prince's arrival created a reshuffle in the order of succession when he displaced his big sister to become second in line to the throne

Hulton Picture Company

BUCKINGHAM PALACE

19 February 1960

The Queen was safely
delivered of a son at 3.30 pm
Today.

Her Majesty and the infant
Prince are both doing well.

John Scott/Camera Press

'Not always a little ray of sunshine'

THE QUEEN ON ANDREW

more secure sense of his mother being there for him than Charles and Anne did, something that has helped shape his character.

Out of the public eye

Few official pictures of Prince Andrew were published and he was rarely seen in public. Not surprisingly, rumours soon started that there was something wrong with him. Shortly after reading a version of these in a magazine, Elizabeth took Andrew, aged 16 months, on to the balcony at Buckingham Palace to watch the fly-past after the Trooping the Colour in 1961. It could be seen that he was a healthy, sturdy child. She was clearly proud of him. 'I think children always do better if they are born with the spring and summer ahead of them,' she had said of her second son.

Andrew was also bright and enquiring. His grandmother commissioned the sculptor Franta Belsky to make a portrait of him in bronze when he was three. 'I want it done before he loses the look of babyhood,' she said. While she worked, the sculptor gave Andrew some clay to play with. 'I have never seen such sustained concentration and excitement of discovery in a child,' she said. He was already showing the confidence of an indulged younger child. When she asked him how old he was he replied, 'Three and a big bit!'

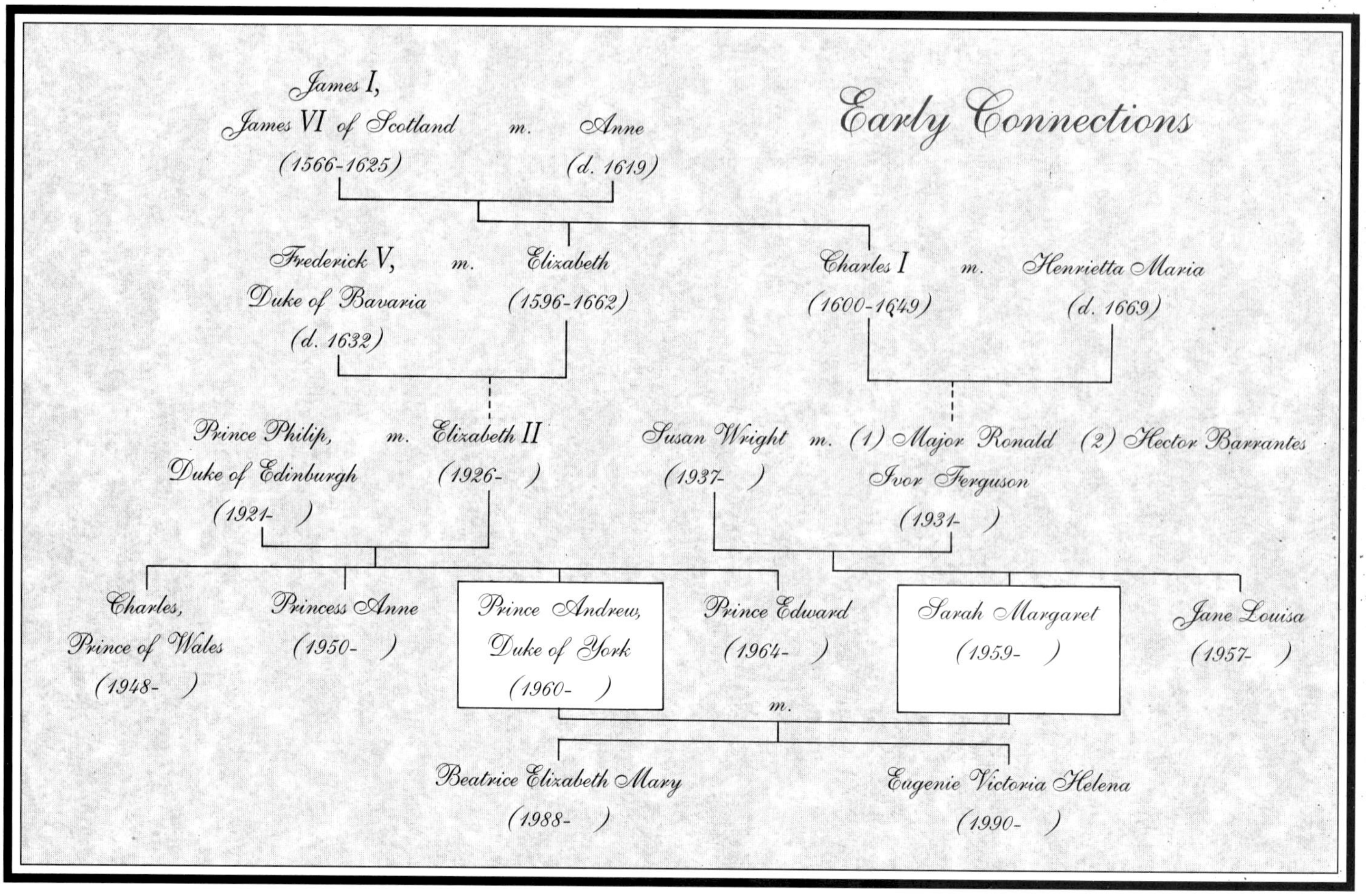

was sitting up in bed reading 'the boxes' a few hours after Prince Andrew was born. As he grew older, she used to let him bring his toys into her study while she worked and would take every opportunity to bath the baby and put him to bed herself. Later she was the one who taught Andrew to read. All these simple pleasures that other mothers accept as their right were new and thrilling to Elizabeth, and they also meant that Andrew had a much

Early Connections

James I,
James VI of Scotland   m.   Anne
(1566-1625)   (d. 1619)

Frederick V,   m.   Elizabeth   Charles I   m.   Henrietta Maria
Duke of Bavaria   (1596-1662)   (1600-1649)   (d. 1669)
(d. 1632)

Prince Philip,   m.   Elizabeth II   Susan Wright   m.   (1) Major Ronald   (2) Hector Barrantes
Duke of Edinburgh   (1926-)   (1937-)   Ivor Ferguson
(1921-)   (1931-)

Charles,   Princess Anne   Prince Andrew,   Prince Edward   Sarah Margaret   Jane Louisa
Prince of Wales   (1950-)   Duke of York   (1964-)   (1959-)   (1957-)
(1948-)   (1960-)
                                                    m.

Beatrice Elizabeth Mary   Eugenie Victoria Helena
(1988-)   (1990-)

♛ **Left** *Alone with a lollipop in a side-window of Buckingham Palace, four-year-old Prince Andrew watches the Trooping the Colour. The Queen saw how Charles and Anne had suffered from early exposure to the limelight and was firm that Andrew should grow up in privacy*

♛ **Below** *Andrew (third from left) races towards the ball in a rugger match between the Heatherdown XV and another prep school. The schoolboy Prince is remembered, among other things, for shinning up the school flagpole and tying a shirt to the top*

Andrew's first lessons were at Buckingham Palace, under the tutelage of 'Mispy' who had also taught Charles and Anne. He was joined by three other boys and two girls to make it seem more like school. It was already clear that he was a 'real boy', tough and somewhat arrogant. 'A natural boss,' Prince Philip called him, and the Queen remarked dryly that he was 'not always a little ray of sunshine'.

By the time he was six, Andrew was becoming a handful, teasing the servants (tying their shoelaces together) and instigating all sorts of practical jokes, such as putting bubble bath in the Palace swimming-pool – very different from the almost painful goodness of Prince Charles. Indeed, Charles found his demon little brother occasionally exasperating and also, perhaps, envied him his carefree spirit. 'Just wait till you go to school. Then you'll have to knuckle down,' he told him gleefully.

An unsentimental education

But school was never the ordeal for Andrew that it was for Charles. At eight and a half, he was sent to Heatherdown, a boarding-school close to Windsor Castle. 'The object is to let

sort of thing at Gordonstoun and it was soon knocked out of him. The ribbings he got were unmerciful and he caught on fast. He had to,' a fellow pupil said. But a hardy boy like Andrew took all this in his stride.

In 1976, when he was 16, Andrew joined the Royal party at the Montreal Olympics. The Canadian Prime Minister, Pierre Trudeau, took the opportunity to suggest that Andrew should spend some time at school in Canada – in the same way that Prince Charles had spent almost a year in Australia. The suggestion was accepted and Andrew started at Lakefield College School in Ontario in 1977.

Sowing the Royal oats

At this age, Andrew was at his most good-looking and the adoring Canadian press had already made much of his Hollywood features. Asked what he thought about the fact that the Canadian press had labelled him Prince Charming, Andrew said, 'Goodness. No comment. That's too dangerous.' But he looked excited and thrilled. 'Girls? I like them as much as the next guy,' he was also quoted as saying, and it wasn't long before he showed that he was

♛ **Right** *Home for the holidays. Andrew relaxes on the moors at Balmoral, his charming, impish grin illustrating a fellow pupil's remark that the younger Prince was 'sometimes a bit of a handful!'*

him lead as normal a schoolboy life as possible,' the headmaster was quoted as saying, and Andrew settled in without any problem.

After Heatherdown, Andrew followed in his father's and elder brother's footsteps and went to Gordonstoun. It had changed since Charles's day – showers were no longer cold, and the school now accepted girl pupils. 'There was a bit of "I am the Prince" about him when he first arrived. But you can't get away with that

Hulton Picture Company

👑 **Above** *Like father, like son. Andrew followed in his father's footsteps by continuing the naval tradition. Pictured here with the Duke aboard* Yeoman *at Cowes in 1973, the face of the man who fought in the Falklands War can already be seen emerging in the 13-year-old Prince*

👑 *Andrew kept up the action-packed pace even in the holidays. During his final year, the Prince spent two weeks on a training course at RAF Brize Norton right after which he parachuted from a Hercules. 'Of course I was nervous,' he admitted, '... but I'm dead keen to do it again'*

planning to live up to his newly acquired nickname: 'Randy Andy'.

There was a school dance shortly after he arrived at Lakefield, and Andrew invited a girl he had met at the Montreal Olympics – Sandi Jones, the daughter of the man who organized the Olympic yachting events.

'I was flabbergasted,' Sandi was reported as saying when this innocent invitation made her famous all over the world. 'I guess we took a shine to each other when we met at the Olympics. I had not expected to hear from him again so soon.'

They met a number of times after this, and Sandi was obviously struck by her glamorous boyfriend. 'He's absolutely great and we get on fabulously. There sometimes wasn't much romancing under the eye of Andrew's bodyguards, though we managed to give them the slip on occasions,' she said in a rush of confidence (something she probably regretted later). 'Andrew can be extremely resourceful. He's just an ordinary guy who wants to have a

fun time with his girlfriend.'

Back in England, Andrew continued to hone his Randy Andy image. He regularly invited girls to stay with him during the holidays from Gordonstoun. Rumours about each 'romance' became so fevered that it was felt necessary to issue a statement to the press: 'He brings friends home with him every holiday,' it ran, soothingly. 'Naturally, like any other boy of his age, he wants his family to meet them.' But the reputation acquired so early would prove hard to shake off.

An ambition achieved

In 1978, Andrew achieved one of his great ambitions: after being measured at school he ran round exulting, 'Guess what – I'm a whole bloody inch taller than my brother! It's the happiest day of my life!'

Andrew did not become Guardian (head boy) as his father and elder brother had done at Gordonstoun, though he was cricket captain. He left school having passed six '0' levels and three 'A' levels but, unlike Charles, he had decided against university. He was set on pursuing a career in the services as a naval pilot. In September 1979, he entered Britannia Royal Naval College in Dartmouth. He graduated in April 1980, after which he was sent to Florida to join the commando ship *Hermes*.

Hulton Picture Company

'CHEERFUL AND FULL OF FUN'

Sarah Margaret Ferguson was born on 15 October 1959 at 9.03 am at the Welbeck Clinic in Marylebone, London. Her father, Major Ronald Ferguson, was a Guards' officer who in time came to command the Sovereign's Escort of the Household Cavalry, and was nicknamed 'the General'. As such he was a friend of the Queen's, a relationship consolidated by the fact that he played polo with Prince Philip, and eventually became Charles's polo manager. Sarah's mother, Susan (née Wright) also had Royal connections, the Wrights being related to most of the first families of Britain. She herself was presented to the Queen at one of the last court débutante presentations in 1955.

They had married when Susan was still a teenager, and their first daughter, Jane Louisa, was born about two years later; Sarah two years after that.

Sarah was 'a very good child, always cheerful and full of fun', her father has said.

Well brought up

Both girls were brought up to be exquisitely polite. They would 'talk to the cowman and ploughman in the same polite way as they would to members of their own family,' a villager remembered; and a nanny has said, 'My first impression of the children was that they were so well behaved. They never caused the slightest trouble. Sarah was always my favourite, she was just so good and so gentle, even as a little girl.' The nanny gave Sarah the affectionate

Camera Press

👑 **Above right** *A chubby and contented Sarah at about 18 months, clutching a furry toy rabbit. 'Mr Rabbit' was a bedtime favourite with both the little Ferguson girls and was the cause of a few squabbles. While Jane was two years her senior, it was usually Sarah who won!*

'Girls? I like them as much as the next guy'

ANDREW

John Scott/Camera Press

'ANDREW'S HAREM'

Sarah Johnson was the first of the long line of pretty young women Andrew was photographed with in his bachelor days. He embarked on his career as 'Prince Charming' at the age of 16 when he attended the Commonwealth Games in Canada and was snapped with Sarah, but later he dated his official escort at the Montreal Olympics, Sandi Jones. The last of the girlfriends, collectively dubbed 'Andrew's Harem', was the lovely American Koo Stark

nickname 'My little Redhair'.

But the gentleness only went so far: the nanny recalls Sarah winning battles with Jane. 'She had that strength of character about her,' she said. 'She was much livelier than Jane.'

Polo and Princes

With a father who lived and breathed polo it was usual for Sarah to spend a lot of time around polo players. As young as three, Sarah was a good rider. She also became used to meeting daddy's friends and their children – who happened to include Prince Charles, Princess Anne, and the little Prince Andrew (four months her junior).

'They met on the polo ground – but doesn't everyone?' Sarah's mother said many years later, when everyone was trying to pinpoint the moment the romance began. 'Our families would meet and naturally the children would play together – they wouldn't understand what royalty meant at that age.'

Sarah learned to ski when she was four. 'She always goes straight down – bang!' her father has said. 'She always has done, not particularly elegantly, but dead straight.'

At the age of five, Sarah went to Daneshill Prep School, Basingstoke, then Hurst Lodge, Sunningdale, in Berkshire.

In 1966, Major Ferguson inherited Dummer Down House in Hampshire, with 800 acres of farmland. He resigned his commission to tend his land, and Sarah was moved to

Daneshill House as a weekly boarder. It was at this school she was given the nickname 'Seconds', because she so often had another helping of school dinners.

Appetite for life

Sarah worked this off as much as possible at sport: tennis, netball, rounders and swimming; and continued to spend as much time as she could riding. When the school changed premises, Sarah and Jane returned to Hurst Lodge as weekly boarders. One of Sarah's closest friends here was Florence Belmondo, daughter of French film star Jean-Paul Belmondo. In common with many of Sarah's school friends, she continues to be a friend to this day.

Life had been very jolly for Sarah, but this was to change in 1973, when she was 13. This was when her mother left her father for Hector Barrantes, the Argentinian professional polo player. The girls were devastated. Major Ferguson said, 'I've never been an over-indulgent father. I wouldn't attempt to compensate for the trauma of the break-up. I set out to be the reverse. I thought it would be a ghastly mistake to compensate financially ... I knew whatever I did I had to stand Sarah and Jane on their own two feet. I tried desperately not to spoil them and I think I succeeded.'

Divorce is hard for children at any time,

👑 **Above left** *Daddy's little girl. Baby Sarah, aged ten months, sits on the Major's lap in a family snap taken on the banks of the Thames. Even at this age, Sarah is very much her father's daughter, down to the topknot of red hair*

👑 *Sarah was a keen and competent rider from very early girlhood.* **Above right** *Competing in a gymkhana on the beloved pony, the replacement for the tiny Shetland on which her mother led the little girl gently round the grassy paddock almost as soon as she could walk*

👑 **Right** *A snap from the Ferguson family album, showing Sarah aged nine with her mother and sister. Sadly, the family was to be widely separated. The divorce took Susan to Argentina as Mrs Barrantes, while Jane grew up to become Mrs Makim and move to Australia. Sarah's wedding was the first family reunion for ten years*

'Nobody ever forgot Sarah'

A TEACHER

All pictures Camera Press

but Sarah was at an age when her confidence was at a low ebb anyway. She had decided she was ugly: she was slightly overweight, had freckles and no boyfriend in sight. 'She was terribly insecure and desperately wanted to be liked,' Jill Adams, a schoolfriend, remembered. 'In fact, everyone did like her, she was the nicest person that I met.'

This popularity didn't help her to feel any better about the way she looked: 'I don't think I'll ever get married. I can't imagine anyone wanting me,' she confided in a friend.

At about this time, a schoolfriend of hers, Sarah Alexander, left to go to Gordonstoun. They had a party for her, and all the friends wrote farewell messages in her book. Florence Belmondo wrote: 'Good luck with the boys!!!' Sarah's message was longer: 'Good Scottish luck!! Mind Prince Andrew! Lots of love, Sarah Fergie (Ferguson) XXXXX'

Head girl

Like Andrew, Sarah had not grown out of playing practical jokes at this age and she liked boisterous games such as pillow fights. But there was something wholesome and pleasant about her jokes, and her spirited reputation did not stop the school appointing her joint head girl. 'They have made you head girl because you are responsible,' her father said proudly

(and somewhat hopefully). It was evidence to him that, despite his divorce, things had turned out all right for Sarah.

'No, daddy,' she told him, 'that's not right. I was so uncontrollable they had to make me head girl so I would start behaving.' This was patently not true. Sarah was either joking or being self-deprecating and modest: 'We have so many girls coming and going that it is easy to forget them,' one teacher has said, 'but nobody ever forgot Sarah.'

Looking to the future

Sarah was moderately successful academically; she gained six 'O' levels and two CSEs. But when it was suggested that she take 'A' levels, Sarah drew the line. 'What? 'A' levels? You must be joking!' she said, and the school did not press her.

Her headmistress has sometimes thought that things might have been different had Sarah been able to read the future: 'I wonder if she would have attended to her history lessons better if she had realized we were talking about the ancestors of her future family!'

Three years after Sarah's mother left the family, her father married again. His second wife was also called Susan. Although she never took Sarah's mother's place, both Sarah and Jane were delighted when the second Mrs Ferguson had three children of her own: Sarah's half-brother Andrew and her two half-sisters, Alice and Eliza.

During Sarah's last term at school she was longing to leave and to start 'real life'.

PLAY THE GAME

Sarah was badly shaken by her parents' divorce, and close friends have suggested that it left her with a great need for reassurance in love and a desire to be liked by everyone. Her father, Major Ferguson, has described the manner of her mother's departure as 'a bit of a fright, to put it mildly, for everyone'.

Susan left without telling her daughters. Sarah was a weekly boarder, so life for her went on much as usual, but, at home, her father floundered.

The divorce was as civilized as they could make it. A few days after it was finalized, Major Ferguson met his ex-wife's lover, Hector Barrantes, as an adversary on the polo field. The match ended in a draw

Sarah

♛ A contented-looking Sarah, aged three and a half, smiles for the camera *right*

♛ Sarah's mother was a keen horse-woman who rode every day, and her father loved playing polo, so it was only natural that their two daughters would learn to ride early in life. 'When she was little I could put her on anything and say: "Right, go and jump that" and she could,' her mother said of Sarah, who is shown with her first pony at the age of ten *below*

Camera Press

Patrick Lichfield/Camera Press

Family Album

Andrew

Camera Press

Hulton Picture Company

👑 Andrew, aged two, plays with one of the family corgis on a sofa at Windsor Castle *above*. An exuberant toddler, his mischievousness usually charmed those who knew him; he was 'sometimes naughty, never nasty', according to one of his aunts

👑 *Right* Andrew salutes, wearing the uniform of the 1st St Marylebone Pack of the Cub Scouts in 1970. The Wolf Cub pack met weekly in the grounds of Buckingham Palace. Among its members were the sons of a shopkeeper, an upholsterer and a bank caretaker – it was a good way for the young Prince to meet children from other walks of life. He was an enthusiastic scout and formed a school scout cub pack when he went to Heatherdown

♔ *Above* This creation, by milliner Marina Killery, consists of flowers and birds nesting in Sarah's hair. It caused a sensation when she wore it

♔ Sarah has plaited tiny bows of bright yellow ribbon into her hair *above right*. The neat style is perfect for keeping cool on a hot day

♔ *Right* Sarah celebrated the Yorks' trip to Los Angeles in February 1988 with two hairpins stuck into a black straw hat. Black and white tailpieces in the shape of strawberries keep her hair tidy

♔ Three cheers for the red, white and blue: *diamanté* hairclips in the shape of British and American flags grace Sarah's hair on her trip to Los Angeles *far right*

BREAKING THE RULES

The Duchess of York is known for her flamboyant way of dressing. She loves bright colours and outré styles and has the confidence to carry them off. She looks stunning in vivid reds and yellows. Royals rarely wear just black and white, but Sarah, with her shining, flame-coloured hair, stands out in any crowd. It is usually her original hairstyles, though, that most often catch the public's eye – and imagination

Sarah's wedding dress *right* took ten weeks to make. The design, by Lindka Cierach, delighted Sarah: 'There will never be a dress to match it,' she exclaimed. The tight-waisted gown is made of ivory-coloured silk duchess satin. The fitted, boned bodice is lavishly decorated with pearls and beadwork. It has bows on the shoulders, and comes to a point front and back. The long, sweeping train falls from a fan-shaped bow at the back of the skirt

Bouquet of lillies, roses, gardenias and a sprig of myrtle for luck

Silk net veiling edged with embroidered scallops and bows

155,000 beads, pearls, sequins and stones were used in all

Lynne Robinson

John Shelley

♔ Sarah's evening-gown *left* was designed by Elizabeth and David Emanuel, the couple who made Princess Diana's wedding dress. The boned black silk-satin bodice contrasts dramatically with a full skirt of white organza embroidered with a black floral pattern

Black braid stitched in scroll patterns adorns jacket, hat, collar and ½ belt at back

Jacket has full-length puff sleeves

Fitted jacket is through seamed and nipped in at the back waist with a ½ belt

♔ *Right* Edina Ronay designed this striking, Cossack-inspired outfit as part of her 1987 autumn/winter collection, and the Duchess of York has since worn it often. The long, fitted jacket of red Venetian wool is lavishly decorated with black braid scrolls on its bodice, stand-up collar and back half-belt. The back of the jacket is pleated, a fashion feature Sarah likes and that she made popular

♔ This figure-flattering suit in emerald-green silk crêpe de Chine *far right* has a simple round neckline and large brass buttons on its button-through jacket and side-buttoning skirt. The wide belt of green suede matches the outfit perfectly, while the green hat is trimmed with a black band and edging which picks up the black of her shoes and gloves

Sun-ray pleated full skirt, ankle-length in Venetian wool

Outfit completed with black opaque tights and black high-heeled court shoes

Jacket, padded at shoulders, and finished at front with a top-stitched button-band

Set-in sleeves finished with top-stitched cuff-band

Knee-length fitted straight skirt with side-front top-stitched button-band

LOVES AND CAREERS

**CHOOSING TO BECOME A HELICOPTER PILOT WAS NO EASY OPTION:
ANDREW SERVED – WITH NO SPECIAL TREATMENT – IN THE
FALKLANDS CAMPAIGN AND RETURNED HOME A HERO.
MEANWHILE, SARAH'S VIVACIOUS PERSONALITY LED HER THROUGH
A SERIES OF JOBS AND AT LEAST TWO SERIOUS ROMANCES**

♛ Andrew is surrounded by his RAF mates below after receiving his wings. The skills that he learned in training were soon put to the test when Britain decided to reclaim the Falkland Islands, where, throughout the campaign, the Prince was in the thick of the action

P RINCE ANDREW'S NAVAL TRAINING SERVED to confirm his feeling that he had chosen the right course. In 1980 he entered the Navy on a 12-year commission and immediately began to train as a helicopter pilot.

He was generally popular, as he had been at school, but some of his mates found him slight-

ly overbearing. 'He played the great "I am" all the time,' complained one of them during his training period. Few of the others seemed to mind how 'H' (an abbreviation of HRH) behaved, and they put him down just as they would any of their fellows: once, when a reporter tried to get him to talk about his love life and he said, 'I don't believe I've ever been in

Hulton Picture Company

love,' a fellow midshipman chipped in, 'Except, of course, with yourself.'

The disciplined life at sea suited Andrew, and his superiors thought well of him. His pleasure in attracting the attention of the press had rather worn off now that he was in his 20s, though he was prepared to concede, 'My only vice is women.' The most irksome part of being who he was was the aggravation of being followed all the time by his security man or the press. 'The security thing is becoming a bit of a bore. My detective's an excellent fellow, but it's a little uncomfortable having to be accompanied everywhere,' he said.

From feeling rather competitive with his older brother, Andrew had come round to thinking that Charles was welcome to the press attention. When Charles visited India in 1980, Andrew said, 'He'll probably drag along a lot of those newspaper chaps and perhaps I'll get a bit of peace.'

Winning his wings

There was nothing about service life that Andrew did not like. He even enjoyed the combat and survival course of the Royal Marines. 'He is strong, physically fit, but, more important, he has determination,' the Commander General said.

After completing his elementary flying training, Andrew moved on to the Royal Naval air station at Culdrose in Cornwall to begin his training as a helicopter pilot. At the end of the course he gained his wings, and won the silver salver for the midshipman with the highest marks. His father, as Admiral of the Fleet, made the presentation. 'Congratulations, good luck and happy landings,' he said proudly.

As a qualified helicopter pilot, Andrew was promoted to the rank of sub-lieutenant and posted to No 820 Squadron operating from HMS *Invincible*. He was very happy. 'When I'm at sea I feel about six inches taller,' he said.

Into battle

In April 1982, when Andrew was 22, Argentina invaded the Falkland Islands, and the *Invincible* set off to help recapture them. There was talk of Andrew being pulled out. But, it was reported from Buckingham Palace, 'He is a serving officer and there is no question in [the Queen's] mind that he should not go.'

As the Falklands operation became more dangerous, there was speculation that Andrew was being kept away from the worst of it, but this was never the case. Indeed, Andrew did everything that the other pilots did: reconnaissance flying, seeking and rescuing survivors and acting as a decoy for enemy missiles, and, at times, he was in great danger.

The Falklands were recaptured on 14 June

1982. The first thing Andrew did was ring his mother. 'She was quite surprised to hear my voice,' he said later. 'Her first words were how proud she was of the armed forces and for me to pass on the message that it had been a marvellous operation.'

The war over, the focus turned to Andrew as a Royal hero. This was a change from being principally interesting for his love-life, and Andrew enjoyed the switch. He stayed on in the Falklands until August, which meant that he

👑 *A tumultuous welcome greeted Prince Andrew and the rest of the crew of the* HMS Invincible *as it docked at Portsmouth. At the front of the crowd were members of the Royal Family, including the Queen who had brought her son a basket of red roses. In a playful gesture, Andrew placed the stem of a rose between his teeth* above

Syndication International

Syndication International

♛ *The Prince spent his 24th birthday at the Royal Opera House in Covent Garden with 21-year-old Carolyn Herbert* right, *daughter of Lord Porchester, the Queen's racing manager. Andrew was, at this time, one of Britain's most eligible bachelors, which meant that every detail of his love life was closely charted by the press*

♛ *The most publicized and serious of Andrew's affairs before he met Sarah was his relationship with the American-born actress, Kathleen Dee-Anne Stark, known as Koo* below. *While she was liked by Andrew's family and – unlike Charles – it wasn't necessary for Andrew to marry a woman with an untainted past, the fact that Koo had appeared in a soft-porn film* was unacceptable

Hulton Picture Company

was away when Prince William was born. 'Now I'll be able to have more privacy,' he said, believing that now he was no longer second in line to the throne, he would be less interesting to the people and the press.

The experience of war had changed him profoundly. 'I'm not looking forward to going back to being a prince,' he said – a very different view from his statement a few short years before that he liked his Royal status.

Andrew couldn't have been more wrong about being less interesting to the press. He returned to Portsmouth on 17 September 1982 to find crowds of people and reporters. On his return, he was awarded the South Atlantic Medal. 'I feel different, but whether I sound, look or am different is for anyone to find out,' he said, more sombre than he had ever been before.

Fired by pictures of him at Portsmouth being surrounded by eager girls – and holding a red rose between his teeth – it was inevitable that someone would ask Andrew what he wanted his future wife to be like. 'The honest answer is that I don't know what I'm looking for yet, simply because I haven't had any chance to

'I'm not looking forward to going back to being a prince'

ANDREW AFTER THE FALKLANDS WAR

think about it,' he replied. 'I know that if I do find somebody, then it is going to come like a lightning bolt and you're going to know it there and then.'

Behind the lens

Life continued to go on in much the same way for Andrew after this, though he was more discreet about his private life. He had also discovered a hobby which began to obsess him: photography. He was given lessons by his uncle, Lord Snowdon, and converted a bathroom at Buckingham Palace into a dark-room. He began to exhibit his work and had much of it published – some of it in a book entitled *Photographs by Prince Andrew*.

♛ *During his 1985 trip to Canada, Andrew stops to talk to a group of children in Nova Scotia left. Canada harbours many fond memories for the Prince and is a country he returns to often*

Anwar Hussein

Andrew's hobby was not particularly well tolerated in the family: 'My family always cringe when they hear the sound of a motor-drive camera, even if it is mine,' he said.

Being a photographer also meant that he met many beautiful women – and some of them became girlfriends. He seemed to fall in love frequently, but only one of his relationships was serious: this was with Koo Stark, an actress. They were very well suited, but the relationship was doomed for a number of reasons: she was American and she was four years older than he. But worst of all, in common with other pretty young actresses making their way, she had helped her career along in the early days by appearing in a soft-porn film. When news of the romance broke, the press had a field day.

An unsuitable romance

It is said that they met in the nightclub Tramp in 1982 when Koo approached Andrew's group and told them they were making too much noise. They soon fell deeply in love. They wrote to each other throughout the Falklands campaign, and afterwards he took her off for a holiday at Princess Margaret's villa on Mustique. Back home, Prince Andrew once dressed up as a milkman to outwit the press and meet Koo at a friend's house, and because of the success of this, on another occasion he dressed up as a traffic warden.

PRINCE OF WAR

Andrew was not spared dangerous missions in the Falklands. One of his duties was to act as a decoy for enemy missiles. He described it thus: 'The helicopter is supposed to hover near the rear of the carrier, presenting a large radar target to attract the missile. The idea is that the Exocet comes in low over the waves and is not supposed to go above a height of 27 feet. So when the missile is coming at you, you rise quickly above 27 feet and it flies harmlessly underneath. In theory.'

At times, he knew real terror. 'When you are in your anti-flash gear and are told to hit the deck because the ship is under attack there is nothing worse,' he said. 'You can only lie there and wait and hope. It's a most lonely feeling.' But he developed ways of dealing with this, and told himself, 'I'm going to survive this.'

An Exocet destroyed the ship *Atlantic Conveyor*, and Andrew and his team hovered over it winching members of the crew to safety while enemy shells came close. 'I saw it being struck by the missile and it was something I will never forget,' he said. 'It was horrific. At the same time I saw a 4.5 shell come quite close to us. I saw my ship *Invincible* fire her missiles. It is not much fun having one of those fellows pick you out as a target. Normally I would say it was spectacular, but it was my most frightening moment of the war'

Hulton Picture Company

👑 **Right** *With her fine features and a mane of curly red hair, Sarah grew into a very pretty young woman. And despite her fears, as a teenager, that she would never appeal to anyone, her looks and her outgoing and fun-loving personality soon began to attract men. In fact, she met her first boyfriend, Kim Smith-Bingham, shortly after leaving school*

Camera Press

👑 **Below** *Sarah was very much in love with Paddy McNally, the man she called 'the Toad', and felt that if she tried her hardest he would someday marry her. And while Paddy enjoyed Sarah's obliging attention, he was not prepared to commit himself to anyone. But he always thought highly of Sarah, later describing her as 'a girl in a million' and adding that 'anyone would be lucky to go out with her, let alone marry her'*

Alan Davidson/Alpha

base, a small ranch 300 miles south of Buenos Aires. It was here she met – and developed a crush on – Kim Smith-Bingham, the brother of a schoolfriend.

Once back in London, she enrolled in the Queen's Secretarial College in Kensington to acquire some basic office skills. And basic was exactly what they were: she and a friend giggled their way through the course and passed out joint last. Her end-of-course report read: 'Bright, bouncy redhead. She's a bit slapdash, but has initiative and personality which she will use well to her advantage as she gets older.'

Sarah was living with a cousin and having a thoroughly good time. She was now romantically involved with Kim, who was back in London too, and working in the City, but some friends thought that she was never very serious about him. When something better came along, such as going to stay with her sister in Australia, she was happy to leave him behind.

Happy temps

Despite her slow secretarial speeds, Sarah was picking up work. Her first job was at Flatmates Unlimited, a flat-sharing agency in Earls Court. 'She was bubbly, helpful, good with people,' said Wendy Keith, her boss. But Sarah only stayed for four months before leaving to work for a public relations company owned by a friend of her father's. He was Peter Cunard who, among other things, organized the Berkeley Square Balls.

Kim tired of the City after a while, and went to work for a designer ski-wear company in the Swiss resort of Verbier. Sarah would fly over to stay with him whenever she could. As he earned very little, she would have to work to keep them going. She took jobs as a chalet maid or baby sitter and helped him make extra commission by selling ski-wear along with him. This spartan existence was relieved by frequent visits to 'the Castle', a chalet part-owned by Paddy McNally, a former rally driver and journalist on the magazine *Autosport*. He was separated from his wife and lived with his two young sons, Sean and Rollo.

Aborted plans

In 1980, Sarah turned 21, and her father's present was a ticket to Argentina and enough money to allow her to tour South and North America. She gave in her notice and flew out to join her mother before embarking on her tour with a friend.

Unfortunately, they did not get very far. They stopped at a ski resort in Squaw Valley, USA, where they took jobs in a mountain café to make money. Here, Sarah had an accident, badly hurting her ankle in a fall. That put paid to the travelling and she had to return to England. She

Andrew desperately hoped his family would accept Koo despite her past, and he took her to meet them at the traditional family gatherings at Balmoral and Sandringham. In fact, the Royal Family *did* like her but, sadly, that was not enough. He was gently discouraged from continuing the relationship, and it was made clear to him that he would not be given permission to marry her.

Bright, bouncy redhead

Sarah left school in 1976 and immediately went to live with her mother and her step-father, Hector Barrantes, for six months at their winter had given up her flat as well as her job for the trip so, while feeling dispirited and in pain, she had to sort her future out.

As far as Sarah was concerned, she was still attached to Kim. But when she made one of her customary trips to join him she found that he had fallen in love with someone else.

Sarah was very upset and her confidence was shattered – but someone was pleased. Paddy McNally had clearly had his eye on her during her visits as his dinner guest in Verbier, and shortly after Sarah had broken up with Kim, he turned up in London and asked her out.

Although he was old enough to be her father and not very good-looking (Sarah nicknamed him 'the Toad'), Paddy had a lot of charm and his wooing was just what she needed with her confidence at such a low ebb.

It was a strange relationship, lived at great distances and largely out of suitcases. Sarah was based mainly in London, but Paddy's business interests took him all over Europe. More often than not, he was in Geneva or Verbier or somewhere on the Grand Prix circuit. Sarah joined him when she could, but, initially, she was tied down by her job with a video company.

After a while, the company closed down, which left Sarah freer to travel with Paddy. She became very fond of his two small sons and enjoyed the time she spent with them. She also became Paddy's official hostess at the Verbier 'castle', where she got to know his set, which included aristocrats and businessmen.

It was a pleasant, if shallow, life. They all rose late for a large breakfast after which the morning was spent skiing. Lunch was at an expensive restaurant, and later Sarah would supervise the lavish dinners at the chalet.

A losing battle

All this food was not particularly good for Sarah's figure, and Paddy was amused by her constant efforts to keep the weight off. He used to tease her about her cranky diets – one week, no red wine, another week, the 'potato-free regime' – while she would be secretly snacking from the refrigerator.

After dinner, the party would take off for a local discothèque, where Paddy had his own table. There, Sarah once dumped a bucket of iced water over his head when he flirted with a pretty girl in front of her.

This was not a one-off occurrence. Sarah was faithful and longed for security. She would have liked nothing better than to marry and settle down, but this was not what Paddy had in mind at all. He liked women and didn't see why he should confine himself to just one.

A new door opens

Paddy, who was fond of Sarah, wanted the best for her. He used his influence to get her a job as London agent for a fine art publishing business. She was made commissioning editor and a director of the company. This was the most demanding job she had ever had: she was responsible for liaising with authors and photographers, overseeing publications and setting up new books. Even so, it was not a full-time job, and it left her plenty of time to travel to Verbier to be with Paddy and go skiing.

There is no knowing how long this might have continued if Sarah had not been invited by her great friend, Diana, the Princess of Wales, to spend Ascot week 1985 as a guest of the Queen at Windsor Castle.

Paddy knew that Prince Andrew would be a member of the house party, but he had never heard Sarah speak particularly well of him – she dismissed him as a 'big head who thinks a lot of himself'. Pleased for Sarah, Paddy offered to drive her to Windsor Castle himself.

LONELY PRINTS

After his return from the Falklands War, Prince Andrew took up photography with obsessional enthusiasm and soon began to exhibit and publish his work. The photographs, such as the eerie image *below* of actress Finola Hughes entitled *The 9th Wife – Dungeons Windsor*, were strange and rather chilling: dark passages, ruined castles, bleak landscapes and ominous skies. Women were shown as distant or unreal. 'I have noticed one or two of them that are interestingly strange . . . I dare say the theme, for some strange reason, is loneliness,' he said of the pictures

Camera Press

'*She's a bit slapdash, but has initiative and personality which she will use well to her advantage as she gets older*'

AN END-OF-COURSE REPORT
ON SARAH

Bryn Colton/Camera Press

♛ *A pregnant Princess Diana and Sarah share a laugh at the polo grounds at Windsor* above *in 1982. Diana, who originally wanted Sarah as a lady-in-waiting, probably saw her old friend as an ally at court. Diana's friendship would be a major factor in the development of Andrew and Sarah's romance*

THE DUKEDOM OF YORK

There have been 14 holders of the title Duke of York since it was first conferred in 1385. In more recent times, the Dukedom of York has traditionally come to be associated with the reigning sovereign's second son. However, a dukedom is not a career and therefore Prince Andrew will, most likely, continue with his naval life for the foreseeable future. The York title does not claim any specific regalia and, since Andrew and Sarah are relatively new to the Family Firm, they have only just begun to build up their own collection of royal heirlooms

Anwar Hussein

Hulton Picture Company

👑 *Far left* The Duchess of York wears a cluster design, three-piece diamond suite consisting of necklace, earrings and bracelet (not seen) during the 1989 tour of Canada. The suite, which made its first appearance on her wedding day, along with the stunning diamond tiara, was a wedding gift to the new Duchess

👑 Sarah's engagement ring *left* is a unique creation which features a large oval Burma ruby surrounded by ten drop diamonds and set in an 18-carat yellow and white gold band. It was designed by Prince Andrew and the team from Garrards, the Royal jewellers, and was valued at £25,000 at the time of the engagement

👑 The arms of the Duke and Duchess of York *above* are, in fact, a modification of Prince Andrew's Royal armorial bearings which now include Sarah's own family coat of arms – a bee and thistle design created by Sarah herself

👑 Prince Andrew wears the ceremonial day dress uniform of a naval lieutenant *right*. Around his neck is the insignia of the CVO (Commander of the Grand Victorian Order) and on his right shoulder are the aiguillettes of personal aide-de-camp to the Queen. The two medals at his left shoulder are the Jubilee Medal (right) and the South Atlantic medal (left), with a rosette denoting that he served in the Total Exclusion Zone in the 1982 Falklands War

Terence Donovan/Camera Press

HIGH JINKS

HAVING MET WHEN THEY WERE CHILDREN AND THROUGH THEIR ADOLESCENCE MEANT THERE WAS NO AWKWARDNESS WHEN THE TWO ATTRACTIVE ADULTS MET AGAIN: FUN AND FLIRTATION WERE THE ORDER OF THE DAY

SARAH WAS PROBABLY READY TO HAVE HER mind changed about Andrew. Certainly her relationship with Paddy had hit a low in June 1985 and, although they superficially continued to have fun together, underneath, there ran a current of sadness and anxiety.

The family party at Windsor had an atmosphere of simple fun – and Andrew's flirtatious puppyishness must have seemed very welcoming after Paddy's worldly-wise sophistication, which was starting to hurt Sarah and sap her confidence. Wise after the event, both of them pinpointed one dinner during that week as being particularly significant. On the face of it, they were just two old acquaintances larking around. 'He made me eat chocolate profiteroles, which I didn't want to eat at all,' Sarah said. The profiteroles were Andrew's own: 'I then didn't have any,' he said. 'So I got hit.'

'Very hard!' Sarah agreed.

'And it started from there,' Andrew said.

For Sarah, used to being teased by Paddy about her weight, Andrew's impish force-feeding of her bore out what his whole manner suggested: he found her very attractive just as she was. The little skirmish showed them both that there was a strong sexual chemistry between them, a current that ran under the playfulness – something that soon became obvious to outsiders.

Opinions revised

But, for Sarah, a week in Andrew's company showed her that there was another side to Andrew. He was more adult, more serious and more sensitive than she had hitherto noticed during her brief meetings with him. The Falklands had changed something fundamental in him and the forced end of his relationship with Koo Stark had also added to the vulnerability. Sarah had to revise her view of Andrew as a bumptious bighead. The fact that he was able to let off steam in an uninhibited, childish way merely diverted attention from the fact that underneath he was far more complex and unsure than most people suspected.

'There are always humble beginnings,' Prince Andrew has said of this fateful dinner. 'It's got to start somewhere.'

♛ **Below** *Andrew and Sarah at* ***Ascot in 1985. This was the week when, even if the lightning bolt did not strike, there was certainly electricity in the air. A familiar friendship quickened into sharper interest as each realized that the childhood companion had grown into something more***

Glenn Harvey/Camera Press

After Ascot week, Sarah flew off as arranged to spend time with Paddy and friends in Ibiza. Sarah was, apparently, her usual self, throwing herself uninhibitedly into the fun. But there was something subtly different in her manner.

She didn't seem quite so eager to please Paddy, and his teasing of her seemed to rankle in a way that it hadn't before. When he made fun of her in front of friends on the occasion that her bikini bottom came off during a high dive, she became openly angry instead of smiling and pretending not to care, as she usually would have. The contrast between his casual treatment of her after the admiring attentiveness of Andrew struck home. Even though at that time she could not believe that anything serious was going to develop between herself and Andrew, she knew he had given her back her self-respect.

The new girlfriend

Andrew was not going to let matters rest there with Sarah, and he began calling her regularly, even though she was still seeing Paddy. He had probably been advised not to give up hope by Diana, who would have known how rocky Sarah's relationship with Paddy had become.

At some time during late 1985, Sarah and Paddy finally broke up. This left the field clear for Andrew, who was not slow to move in, and the press were not slow to pick up on the fact that 'Fergie' was a new girlfriend.

> ## 'Sarah knew intuitively that she and Andrew were right for each other'
>
> ONE OF SARAH'S FRIENDS

Andrew wooed Sarah in the time-honoured fashion. Tickets for the ballet were followed by dinner for two at Buckingham Palace. He sent her bouquets of roses and every Friday he would jump into his car and drive the 150 miles from the naval base at Portland to take her out for the evening. Sometimes they went to a club or visited friends, or spent a quiet evening in at Andrew's suite at the Palace.

Fooling the press

Andrew attempted to put the press off the scent by taking out other women – including television personality Selina Scott, but the mystery of that dinner was solved when she was granted an interview with him later that year.

Andrew and Sarah had great success in throwing off the press and they managed to spend a lot of time together. It wasn't long before Sarah was hopelessly in love. Her flatmate, Caroline Beckwith-Smith, knew every nuance of Sarah's feelings. 'Sarah knew intuitively that she and Andrew were right for each other and didn't want anything to spoil it,' she said later. 'As a woman, and something of a romantic, she realized sooner than Andrew. As a member of the Royal Family he is used to covering up his feelings. Perhaps that also means that it was more difficult to peel away his mask and find out what was really going on in his heart.'

During this time, Andrew's interview with Selina Scott went out on television. She referred to the bolt of lightning he had said was necessary to alert him to the fact that he was in

♛ Below *Skiing in style. Sarah joins the Prince and Princess of Wales on their skiing holiday at Klosters in 1986. Diana had spotted the chemistry between her friend and her brother-in-law and quietly promoted the match, making sure that the couple were given every opportunity to explore their growing feelings for each other*

Glenn Harvey/Camera Press

Tim Graham

♛ **Above** *Andrew and Sarah share a joke while watching the polo at Windsor in 1986. The ease of years of friendship, coupled with the well-publicized rumbustious sense of humour, formed a firm foundation for the romance which had suddenly flowered between them the previous summer*

'We are a good team'

SARAH

love. Andrew dodged the issue as best he could. 'One member of my family, who shall remain nameless, suggested that perhaps it was time they saw me with charred ears and I'm only sorry that this evening I didn't come with charred ears,' he said. And when Sue MacGregor asked him on Radio Four's *Woman's Hour* what qualities he would want in a wife, he told her, 'I honestly don't know what I'm looking for.'

Sarah was able to take her mind off the romance by concentrating on her work. She was rushing to complete a book on the Palace of Westminster. The author had fallen ill and she had to take over much of his work as well as her own. On one occasion she left her flat at dawn to take photographs of parts of the Palace to help the author write his text.

Royal weekends

In January 1986, Sarah was invited to spend the New Year break with the Royal Family at Sandringham. It was here that Andrew first mentioned that he was seriously thinking about marriage.

This was what Sarah had been waiting for, and she was thrilled. But, as one friend noticed, she was also scared: 'While she was enormously happy, she was petrified about what she was

letting herself in for.' Sensibly, Sarah asked Andrew to wait a little longer, to give her time to consider.

The Queen and Prince Philip were delighted by the progress of the romance. They invited Sarah to stay at Sandringham again, and Diana invited her to spend a weekend at Highgrove. On 19 January 1986, Andrew set sail for Sweden, taking with him a photograph of Sarah sitting on a bench in the Windsor gardens which he had taken during the great 'week of the profiteroles'.

A couple of weeks later, Andrew's ship docked briefly in the Port of London and Sarah accompanied Diana and Prince William on a tour of the ship. It was Sarah's first official public appearance with members of the Royal Family. 'Keep smiling, for goodness' sake keep smiling,' Diana told her in a whisper loud enough to be heard by the throngs of pressmen.

Proposal at last

Soon after this, Andrew and Sarah spent a weekend together at Floors Castle in Scotland, the home of friends. They had their usual spirited fun: a snowball fight and long walks in the grounds. This was when Andrew proposed again – this time, properly. An interviewer asked Sarah much later if she remembered Andrew's words.

'Absolutely!' she said. ' ... But I'm not telling you!' Did he go down on one knee, the interviewer wanted to know. 'No, both, that I will tell you,' Andrew replied. This time Sarah accepted at once – nervous that she might have left it too late, or that he would change his mind. 'If you wake up tomorrow morning, you can tell me it's all a huge joke,' she said.

Of course Andrew didn't. The teetotal Prince even called for a bottle of vintage champagne to toast their engagement with.

Hulton Picture Company

THE FALSE START

Andrew and Sarah fell in love in 1985 because the time was right. They had had the opportunity two years earlier, when they had both been invited to spend the weekend at Floors Castle, the Scottish home of the Duke and Duchess of Roxburghe (who are shown *below* at a point-to-point with Andrew, Princess Margaret and Viscount Linley).

Andrew had spent a lot of time over the weekend taking pictures of Sarah because he was a newly obsessive cameraman and he loved her mass of fiery curly red hair.

'She was very flattered by the attention,' a friend said, 'but didn't really know what to do for the best.' She was deeply involved with Paddy at the time, and things had not yet soured between them. Andrew, too, was ready to flirt but not to fall in love: his relationship with Koo had not yet burned itself out.

Their playfulness together was quite evident during this weekend, but the sparks between them either were not ignited – or were studiously ignored. During one romping game of hide and seek, Sarah dived in under a table after Andrew and soundly pinched him. 'Steady on,' he yelled. 'You aren't allowed to pinch the royal bottom!'

Camera Press

Andrew designed the engagement ring and had it made up by the Crown jewellers, Garrard. The centre jewel was a fine oval Burma ruby – red for Sarah's hair. Ten drop diamonds were set in a cluster around this and mounted in 18-carat white and yellow gold.

Royal assent

On Saturday, 15 March, Sarah was invited to lunch with the Queen at Windsor Castle, and this was when the Queen formally gave her assent to the match. Andrew's mother was thrilled that everything had worked out so well. As Andrew said later, she was 'overjoyed. Very happy, very pleased ... just as a delighted parent, I think.'

Prince Andrew then had to ask Sarah's father for her hand. 'That was fairly nerve-racking,' Andrew admitted, but Sarah confirmed that her father was as delighted as the Queen had been.

Normally, the engagement would have been announced immediately. But as Budget Day fell on the Tuesday, it was agreed with Downing Street to postpone the announce-

☝ Above *At the Royal Windsor Horse Show in 1986. The Queen is very fond of Sarah and was an unfailing source of support and advice during Sarah's early days as a Royal. Her Majesty was delighted at her second son's choice of bride and, as a mother, must have been relieved to see Andrew happy at last after the strain and unhappiness she suffered over the ending of his affair with Koo Stark*

Above *The ring. Andrew and Sarah proudly show off her unique ruby and diamond engagement ring. It had been commissioned from the Royal jewellers months previously when trays of rings were brought to the Palace along with suggested designs on paper. Andrew refined the designs and the finished ring, judged by experts to be worth at least £25,000, was delivered just two days before the announcement. The jeweller described the ring as being unlike any other in the world*

ment of the engagement until the Wednesday after this.

That Monday, Sarah went to work as usual, though, significantly, she arrived with a police escort. 'I'm not saying anything, but it is a lovely day,' she said to the shouted questions of the press corps. After lunch with her father, Sarah popped in to see the dress designer Alastair Blair to ask him to rush her through a suit for Wednesday and the official announcement. Blair and his team worked through the night to finish the demure dark blue wool crêpe suit with its pleated skirt, wide leather belt and silver buttons.

Officially announced

Sarah then moved into Buckingham Palace, where security (and the press) could be dealt

with as a fact of life.

On the day of the official announcement of the engagement, 19 March 1986, Sarah woke with a tension headache. Her hairdresser, Denise McAdam, turned up at the Palace to do her hair and then she joined Andrew in his study to face the four accredited court correspondents.

'I asked Shea [the Queen's press secretary] to get all you court correspondents together,' Andrew said seriously. 'I wanted to tell you it's all off. It's just a hoax.'

Later, the interview was televised. It was informal and revealing: they touched each other a lot and were plainly in love, and everyone was able to see how high-spirited and delighted with each other they were.

Andrew was asked whether marriage meant he would be settling down. 'No, no,' he replied hastily. 'I mean, I don't see there's anything settling in it. It's a mighty upheaval for most people, and I think it'll be an upheaval for both of us.'

'A good team'

They had obviously talked a lot of things through. 'I think it's worth saying that I have no plans to change my Navy career, on the advice of Sarah,' Andrew said. 'Very strongly,' agreed Sarah. 'We discussed it at some length, and for the foreseeable future I will be continuing my naval career as it is at the moment,' Andrew went on. 'Sarah is quite prepared to put up with that, and I think she will be a remarkable wife if she can.'

'My job enables me to work from home, and I would be able to amalgamate my work with Andrew's career, and be a good wife to Andrew,' Sarah agreed. 'I can cook too. You can do anything you want if you can put your mind to it ... I think it's a case of where there's a will there's a way. I want to make sure I do things properly.'

Sarah was asked what she saw as Andrew's qualities. 'Wit, charm and good looks,' she said emphatically.

The interviewers asked how Sarah was coping with learning the royal ropes. 'Andrew has been a great help to me,' she replied, 'and also the Queen, who has been at the end of a barrage of questions. She has been very long-suffering ... But really it comes down to using your initiative and common sense.'

The interviewers were curious as to why an independent girl was going to promise to 'obey' at the wedding. 'I was thinking of obeying in moral terms, as opposed to physically obeying,' Sarah explained. 'I am not the sort of woman who is going to meekly trot along behind. When I want to, I will stress a point. When we are in a dilemma or situation which needs someone to make a decision it will be Andrew

Hulton Picture Company

who will take the lead. He will make the decision because he is the man of the marriage. Therefore, in that sense, I will obey him at one stage or another.'

'But I promise to worship!' Andrew added.

Happy to marry anywhere

The chosen venue for the wedding was Westminster Abbey, and they were asked what had led them to make this choice. 'We could not really get married in Dummer Church, in Sarah's home village,' Andrew answered. 'We would not have been able to fit everyone in!'

Sarah explained that neither of them really cared about *where* they were to be married: 'Andrew and I would quite happily get married anywhere, because we are marrying ourselves – and not the world.'

Asked how she would feel on her wedding day, Sarah smiled. 'I will be completely and utterly over-excited at the prospect of marrying the man waiting at the top of the aisle,' she said.

Asked the same question, Andrew was stumped. 'I have no idea! But I'll shout the answer to you across the Abbey if you want!'

Two royal jokers

Court Correspondent Tom Corby told afterwards how impressed he had been with Sarah. 'She zings,' he said. 'She absolutely sparkles, I can see why Andrew fell in love with her. They were a double act, two royal jokers in the royal pack . . . There was an air of restrained knockabout during the entire interview.'

It fell to Sarah's father to reveal that it hadn't been as easy for her as it looked. 'It has been quite an ordeal for a country girl,' he said. 'I am extremely proud of her. She has behaved absolutely perfectly, never holding her head down, always being polite, always smiling, yet never giving anything away.'

Everyone in the Royal Family shared his sentiments about his daughter. 'I think she's wonderful – but then I'm biased,' Prince Charles said when asked.

Prince Philip agreed. 'They seem very happy together, are well adjusted, and I think Sarah will be a great asset,' he said. 'She is fortunate to have established an occupation before joining the family and she's capable of becoming self-employed. I hope Sarah will be able to continue as a sort of consultant, and I don't see why anyone should complain about that.'

The usually taciturn Princess Anne added her voice to theirs. 'I think my brother is an exceedingly lucky man,' she said.

The day after the engagement was announced, Sarah went to work as usual. 'I'm not going to change, why should I?' she said, smiling, to the assembled group of reporters and photographers.

👑 *The official engagement photograph* left. *Andrew and Sarah's happiness in each other and their delighted relief at the end of the months of secrecy shine clearly through the traditionally formal pose in the Blue Drawing Room at Buckingham Palace*

👑 *Sarah returned to work the day after the announcement of her engagement* above. *Her unfailing good humour and competent handling of the hordes of reporters who followed and photographed her every move won their respect and admiration. But the strain was enormous and soon Sarah had to move into an office at the Palace and work from there*

ROYAL RESIDENCE

SUNNINGHILL PARK

*The Duke and Duchess of York's new home at
Sunninghill Park in Berkshire – only five miles from
Windsor Castle – is the newest British Royal residence.
The two-storey house, a wedding gift from the Queen, is
built of hand-made red brick, with a steeply pitched
red-tiled roof. Besides 12 bedrooms, there are a cinema, a
billiards and games room, a swimming pool, tennis court
and helicopter pad*

THE NEW PRINCESS

AS SOON AS THE ENGAGEMENT WAS ANNOUNCED, PUBLIC INTEREST WAS INTENSE. WEDDING SECRETS WERE CLOSELY GUARDED BY THE FAVOURED FEW IN THE KNOW BUT, FANNED BY THE PRESS, EXCITEMENT ROUND THE WORLD MOUNTED AS THE WEDDING DAY DREW NEAR

♛ *Sarah's sea-blue silk dress catches the breeze as she makes her début appearance at an event with Andrew in June* left. *By this time the wedding hysteria was reaching a crescendo as the nation watched every move of their future Princess*

♛ *On 14 June, just five weeks before the wedding, Sarah and Andrew watch the Trooping of the Colour from the balcony of Buckingham Palace* below *among an assemblance of Royals. Although not yet married, Sarah was already firmly established as one of the Family, having won over most of its members*

Glenn Harvey/Camera Press

S ARAH'S SUITE AT BUCKINGHAM PALACE WAS the same one Diana had occupied in her days as fiancée, on the second floor. Sarah scarcely spent any time there in the first week, as she excitedly visited friends and relations who were eager to know all the details of the romance that had been kept from the press and public.

Life as a Royal wife-in-waiting was as difficult for Sarah as it had been for Diana. It soon became clear that she could no longer negotiate the press and the crowds to go to work each day. Her determination not to change her daily life was not enough, and Sarah was soon having to use a study overlooking the Mall in Buckingham Palace to work in, rather than her office on the fourth floor of a building in the West End.

Arranging a wedding and contemplating the change it means in your life is hard enough for any bride-to-be, but add to that the hysteria of the press and the reason why Sarah soon felt she had to get away from it all becomes plain. She phoned her friend Florence Belmondo in Antigua and extracted an invitation to stay with her in hopes of leaving the world's photographers behind.

Unfortunately, the press tracked her down even there, but Sarah managed to maintain her good humour and almost boyish high spirits. Once, at a restaurant, she sent the press contingent a bowl of flowers from her table: they responded by sending over a bottle of champagne. On another day, she called to photographers crouching behind some bushes waiting for a bikini shot, 'Don't get sunstroke, boys!' Despite the press attention, Sarah had a real chance to relax, and she returned looking rested, lightly tanned and very pretty.

Shared tastes

On her return, Sarah and Andrew got down to planning their wedding, including drawing up a wedding gift list for their guests. The long list had many expensive items, such as high-quality china and furniture, aimed at richer friends and relations, but it also included small items — such as a teddybear teapot and mugs, pictures of Beatrix Potter animals, and matching tankards bearing their initials.

Their second television interview was even more relaxed than the first. Sarah as 'Fergie' had found herself thoroughly welcomed into the hearts of the press and the people, as well as her husband-to-be's family. Being engaged was also clearly suiting Andrew. The weeks that had passed had given them even more delight in each other and an obvious ease in each other's presence.

They were interviewed sitting on a wall at Andrew's base in Portland. They touched constantly, Andrew once nearly knocking Sarah off the wall with a resounding slap on her back!

Tim Graham

♛ *Sarah waves to the crowds from the Glass Coach as she and her father ride from Clarence House to Westminster Abbey right. In her hair she wears an Edwardian-style wreath of flowers which would later be replaced with a tiara after the signing of the register. This was just one of Sarah's personal touches that made the lavish ceremony a more intimate affair*

♛ *Below Major Ferguson looks on while Sarah and an assistant attempt to arrange her train before the bridal party entered the Abbey. As they began to make their way up the blue carpet to the altar, Sarah turned to her father and joked, 'Do you know the way?' 'I'm following the blue,' was his reply*

John Shelley

John Shelley

They chatted unreservedly about their shared likes – including fish and chips – and Sarah was frank about her full figure, which had started to attract some unfavourable comment from the fashion press.

It says much for Sarah's soft-heartedness that she thought of writing to Paddy's young sons before the wedding, as she had been very close to them at one time. She also made it clear that she was going to remain friends with Paddy – it was generally acknowledged that he made a good friend, even if he was an unsatisfactory partner – and she hoped Andrew would like him too. She introduced the two men during the week of the wedding at a lavish pre-nuptial ball thrown by Major Ferguson at the Guard's Polo Club.

Pre-wedding jokes

As is traditional, Andrew had made arrangements for his stag night prior to the wedding. Sarah, who found the concept rather archaic, hatched a plan with her friend, the comedienne Pamela Stephenson, and Diana. They hired policewomen's outfits and planned to 'raid' the party, which included all their menfolk: Prince Charles and Billy Connolly, as well as the groom and other guests. Unfortunately, they were thwarted because the press had discovered where the party was being held and had staked it out.

Disconsolately they set out in their uniforms for the nightclub Annabels instead, where they ordered some orange juice and discussed strategy. While deep in conversation, they were mistaken for kissogram girls!

They couldn't let the joke spoil, so they cooked up an alternative plan in the club. This time, they decided to lie in wait for Andrew as he drove up to Buckingham Palace in his Jaguar after the party. They halted the car and told Andrew he would have to accompany them to the police station. It was a great success. Bewildered, Andrew couldn't make out in the gloom who they were and he had a few uncomfortable minutes of fast-talking before he caught on to the carefully planned prank.

Duke of York

Shortly before the wedding, it was announced that Andrew was to be made Duke of York, a title last held by his grandfather, George VI. It also meant that Sarah (who would become a princess on marriage) was to be known as the Duchess of York, rather than the rather ugly and cumbersome 'Princess Andrew'.

The Queen actually created Andrew Duke of York, Earl of Inverness and Baron Killyleagh (the County Down home of Sarah's ancestors) only 90 minutes before the ceremony started.

Inevitably, there were nerves before the wedding, and not only for the bride and groom. Diana was nervous about how her naughty little boy, Prince William, chosen to be one of the bridal attendants at the wedding, would behave. 'I'm going to put down a line of Smarties in the aisle of Westminster Abbey so that William will know where to stand – and he's got to stay there,' she said. 'He's terribly excited. I only hope he behaves in the Abbey. He will rise to the occasion – at least I hope he will.'

John Shelley

'I want it to be like something out of Cinderella'

SARAH ON THE WEDDING

The then First Lady of the United States, Nancy Reagan, arrives at the Abbey above. Guests attending the celebrations included a mix of official dignitaries as well as a large number of Andrew and Sarah's friends, including television personalities

Glenn Harvey/Camera Press

THE PRESS TURNS NASTY

Just two weeks after the engagement, 'Fergie' began to see the other side of the press's attention, as they bombarded her with criticism and advice about the way she looked, a fruitful topic that continues to this day.

Andrew thought it was all rubbish, but he helped her as much as he could by vetting her wardrobe and weeding out unsuitable garments. 'For the first few weeks, I rather ran her wardrobe,' he said. Sarah was relieved. 'Clothes are not a priority for me. I am not a great clothes horse but it is a job and it has got to be done.'

She refused to worry about her womanly, rather than model-girl, figure. A woman, she said, should have 'a trim waist, a good up-top and enough down the bottom but not too big . . . I'm quite happy with my figure, quite happy with myself.'

'Naturally she got quite upset at various stages about the criticism – her weight and all that,' her father said. 'But as I explained to her, unfortunately, she's no longer a private person.'

'I'm just going to be me,' Sarah decided in the end. 'To begin with, I made the dreadful mistake of taking in what the fashion people wrote . . . but I don't really want to change. I'm quite happy with myself.'

Andrew agreed, 'You can be so hidebound by fashion that you end up tying yourself in knots,' he said. 'Dress the way you want to dress'

Flanked on either side by family members, Andrew and Sarah exchange their vows above in a traditional service conducted by the Archbishop of Canterbury, Dr Robert Runcie. The generous displays of colourful roses that filled the Abbey and the music provided by the choir, organ and orchestra created a brilliant setting for the magnificent ceremony

Prince William pulls faces at the other attendants above. The long ceremony in the hot Abbey was bound to test his patience but, to his mother's great relief, he behaved well

The new Duchess of York stops to curtsey to the Queen right after signing the register. Her father later referred to the gesture as his 'proudest moment'

A GLORIOUS DAY

It was a wonderful day for a wedding. The marriage – organized by Princess Alexandra's brother-in-law, the Earl of Airlie – took place at Westminster Abbey on 23 July 1986 and went beautifully, as planned. Though just as important to the participants, the wedding was not a state occasion, unlike that of the Prince and Princess of Wales, so the couple were much freer in their choice of guests. A certain number of dignitaries were obligatory, but the couple were also able to invite all their friends. These included Billy Connolly and Pamela Stephenson, the Elton Johns, the Michael Caines, the American comedienne Joan Rivers and David and Lady Carina Frost.

Sarah had been involved with the planning of the wedding every step of the way. She was very specific about what she wanted. 'Lots of roses – and more flowers than at any other Royal wedding,' she had said firmly – and she had got her wish. Roses were in season, and the Abbey was bedecked with them – mainly white and peach Jack Frost roses.

A fairytale wedding

What Sarah wanted to get away from was the overly formal feeling of some royal weddings. 'I want it to be like something out of Cinderella,' she explained, and certainly she made sure that the designer she chose understood that she wanted to look as much like a fairy princess herself as was possible.

She had decided on the designer after talking to her flatmate, Carolyn Beckwith-Smith, whose own stunning wedding gown was being made by the Polish-born designer Lindka

Cierach. 'She is absolutely brilliant,' Carolyn said. 'You go along to her with your own ideas and she quickly tells you what will work and what will not.' This was just what Sarah wanted, and in consultation with Lindka created a gown that was everything she had dreamed.

The closely fitting dress was in an ivory-coloured satin which perfectly suited Sarah's creamy red-head's skin. The intricate bead-work on the bodice and the sleeves was based on Sarah's coat of arms – a honey bee on a this-tle tied with a ribbon and incorporating an 'S' for Sarah. This theme was continued, inter-woven with anchors, waves and hearts, on the seventeen-and-a-half-foot-long train.

Personal touches

A very Sarah touch was the large bow at the back of the dress, and smaller bows on her shoulders. Her shoes, designed by Manolo Blahnik, were made of English silk-satin and embroidered with bows, ribbons and a bee motif.

She came to the altar with her fragile veil over her face, her hair loose and flowing be-neath it. A circlet of lilies of the valley, indi-vidual cream lily petals and clusters of cream roses and gardenias held her veil in place. (This was later replaced by a leaf scroll and diamond tiara mounted in platinum 'borrowed', as in good wedding tradition, from a friend.)

Sarah had eight young attendants. The girls wore outfits that reflected Sarah's own, and the boys echoed the groom's ceremonial naval uni-form in a mixture of 17th-century midshipman

Hulton Picture Company

Hulton Picture Company

John Shelley

dress uniform for the older boys, and Victorian sailor suits for the little ones.

The oldest bridesmaid was seven-year-old Rosanagh Innes-Ker, the daughter of the Duke and Duchess of Roxburghe, at whose castle Andrew proposed to Sarah. Alice Ferguson, Sarah's half-sister, was also a bridesmaid, as was Zara Phillips, Andrew's niece, and Laura Fellowes, Diana's niece. Peter Phillips was one of the older pageboys, and he was helped by

Prince William, Andrew Ferguson (Sarah's half-brother) and Seamus Makim, her nephew.

The first person to see Sarah before she left for the Abbey was her father. As she walked down the carpeted stairway, he recalled, 'It was the most extraordinary vision. I was absolutely bowled over.' He had been very nervous on her behalf, but he soon realized that this was not necessary. 'At that moment I was prepared for anything. Stupid jokes to relax her and so on. As

♛ *Andrew and Sarah emerge from the Abbey arm in arm, followed by their page boys and attendants* below. *The couple's joy is echoed by the pealing of the Abbey's ten bells and recorded for posterity by an army of cameras*

soon as I looked into her face I knew there was no necessity whatsoever to go into any charades to calm her down. There was a serene happiness about her. She was completely relaxed.' Sarah, in fact, was the first one to crack a joke. As she was about to walk down the aisle with her father, she turned to him and said, 'Do you know the way?'

The ceremony was solidly traditional, using the old order of service from the Book of Common Prayer. The Royal Marines played Elgar's *Imperial March*.

Following family tradition, the wedding ring which Prince Edward, as his brother's 'supporter', produced for the groom to give to the bride was made of Welsh gold. The surprise came, though, when Sarah produced a gold band for Andrew to wear.

Despite careful practice, Sarah made one small slip, adding an extra 'Christian' into Andrew's name.

Supremely happy

After the ceremony, the couple looked supremely happy. Sarah, with her veil thrown back, was flushed with the excitement and pleasure as she curtsied to the Queen and turned to walk back up the aisle. Then, in an aside to Andrew, she said, 'I've forgotten to pack my toothbrush!'

As the couple walked down the aisle, Sarah gave her friend Carolyn Cotterell a stage wink and smiled widely at all her friends and relations. (Paddy McNally and Kim Smith-Bingham were among the guests.)

As Sarah and Andrew drove back to Buckingham Palace in their open coach, the cheering crowds drew wider and wider smiles from the pair and especially enthusiastic waves from Sarah, the new Princess.

Back at the Palace, 120 guests sat down to a wedding breakfast of salmon, lamb, strawber-

John Shelley

♛ **Above** *Greeted with hugs and kisses from their attendants, the new Royal couple arrive at Buckingham palace where they began the second half of their wedding day with a lavish breakfast feast shared with 120 guests*

♛ *In between breakfast and the obligatory photo sessions, the Duke and Duchess made repeated balcony appearances. And following the tradition begun by Charles and Diana on their wedding day, Andrew kissed his bride right to the delight of the cheering crowds and the ranks of press photographers*

Anwar Hussein

Both pictures Hulton Picture Company

ries and cream with vintage Bollinger champagne. Using the Duke's ceremonial sword the couple cut the five-tiered wedding cake, made by the Royal Navy Supply School at HMS *Raleigh* in Cornwall.

The new Princess

After a rest the Royal Family made its traditional appearance on the balcony. The crowd roared its pleasure and called for the couple to kiss – just as Charles and Diana had done. 'Kiss her! Kiss her!' came the chant, and initially Andrew and Sarah pretended not to know what was being asked. They cupped their ears and called 'What? We can't hear you!'

The kiss, when it did come, was enjoyed by the cheering crowd as well as a worldwide television audience of 800 million people.

Afterwards, the new Princess and Duchess of York changed into her flowery Suzanne Schneider going-away outfit. Prince William chased the carriage as it took the newlyweds away, and the Queen had to hold him back. It was thought that he wanted to get his hands on the giant teddybear which had been installed on the carriage by Diana and Viscount Linley.

Sarah and Andrew had originally wanted a honeymoon cruise in the Mediterranean, and had planned to fly to the south of France to join the Royal yacht *Britannia*.

But the USA chose this moment to bomb Libya and it was believed that the Royal yacht would be too tempting a target for retaliatory action. Eventually, they flew to the Azores and cruised their way gently back to the Solent.

'A marvellous pair'

There was time for the new couple to be almost entirely alone, and for Sarah to start to absorb the various pieces of advice she had been given by those close to her. Diana's advice on joining the 'Family Firm' was short and sweet: 'be delightful but discreet'.

Sarah's father's advice was similar: 'Be charming, co-operative, but say nothing.'

But Major Ronald Ferguson spoke for everyone with his final verdict. 'I don't see any reason why they shouldn't remain a marvellous pair,' he said. 'They are fun and they go about things in their own way. They're impromptu and outgoing, which shows in practically everything they do . . . Long may it last.'

Amid enthusiastic cheers and a cloud of colourful paper confetti, Andrew and Sarah leave the forecourt of Buckingham Palace above *in their carriage, which was installed with a satellite dish at the back, and – thanks to Diana and Viscount Linley – a giant teddybear in front. Their first stop was to be the Chelsea Hospital. Here, the new Duchess would greet and chat to the residents before the short helicopter flight which was to take her and the Duke to Heathrow airport. They would then board their British Aerospace 146 jet* inset *to fly to the Atlantic islands of the Azores for their honeymoon cruise aboard the* Britannia

THE PERFECT COUPLE

Alone among the royal marriages, that of the Yorks has never attracted the slightest whisper of speculation on its stability. Outwardly confident and extrovert, both Sarah and Andrew have known loneliness and insecurity. Their happiness is based not upon castles in the air but on a down-to-earth, honest, whole-hearted enthusiasm for each other and a determination to build a close and loving family

♛ Sarah wore this dazzling pearl and gold necklace with a gold and diamond pendant *right* to stunning effect with her wedding dress. Many people thought it was a wedding present from the Prince, but in fact it had made its appearance before the big day. The necklace is a favourite piece and the Duchess frequently wore it in public the following year, particularly during her first overseas tours in 1987 when she and Prince Andrew visited Canada and Mauritius

Anwar Hussein

Anwar Hussein

👑 *Left* Fatherhood brought the photographer Duke a whole new subject of endless fascination on which to focus his camera. Andrew took this picture of himself with his wife and daughter when baby Beatrice was less than a month old. The warmth and closeness of the informal family study form a strong contrast indeed with the lonely, brooding mood of many of the Prince's earlier photographs

👑 *Below* Klosters January 1990. Baby Beatrice had held the position of youngest Princess in the Royal Family for 17 months when these pictures of the little girl playing in the snow with her mother were taken. But the Duchess was already seven months pregnant with her second daughter, Princess Eugenie, who would be born just a few weeks later on 23 March in London

Camera Press

👑 *Left* Boating off the idyllic island of Mauritius in the first year of their marriage. Andrew and Sarah had to begin married life in the spotlight of public attention, after only a brief honeymoon. Yet this picture taken on the tour, one of the first of their official engagements as Duke and Duchess of York, shows the newlyweds sharing a moment together in perfect harmony. The obvious warmth between the young couple kept them lighthearted and happy throughout what must have been a testing time and has remained a keynote of their marriage

Tim Graham

THE HOUSE OF YORK

SETTLING INTO A ROYAL MARRIAGE AND COPING WITH LIFE IN THE NAVY AT THE SAME TIME CAN BE DIFFICULT. BUT, SUPPORTED BY THEIR FAMILIES AND WITH A GROWING FAMILY OF THEIR OWN, THE YORKS – WITH GOOD HUMOUR AND HIGH SPIRITS – HAVE ACHIEVED A SUCCESSFUL, ENDURING ROYAL MARRIAGE

ON THEIR RETURN FROM THE HONEYMOON, Sarah and Andrew moved back into Buckingham Palace. While they had been away, her belongings had been moved into Andrew's apartments. They considered the honeymoon all too brief, as Andrew had to return to his ship almost immediately after they came back.

Now Sarah had a real dose of adjusting to her royal status. She was 'Your Royal Highness' and 'Ma'am' to everyone she passed in the corridors of the Palace. With friends, she made it clear that she wanted nothing to change – at least in private. 'Look,' she told a group of her old friends at the first dinner party she went to. 'It's Fergie or Sarah, none of this Your Royal Highness nonsense, okay?'

A serviceman's wife

What she wanted was to have Andrew there, so that she could be able to discuss things with him. She was learning very quickly that it is hard to be a serviceman's wife.

'She found it strange having a husband who had to go off almost from the moment they married, even though she knew what she was in for from the start,' her father said.

Sarah compensated by throwing herself into her work, something she enjoyed anyway. 'I do have two sides. I have an extremely hard-working and thoughtful side too,' she said of herself. 'There are 25 hours in a day. I've proved it! . . . I burn the candle at both ends and I get up far too early, which means . . . my weekends are spent asleep!'

But it wasn't work for work's sake that drove Sarah on. 'I am a service wife first,' she said. Work fulfilled a function within her marriage. 'I want to do it because at the end of the day when Andrew comes back I have actually done something, I haven't just been sitting

♔ With their undisguised enthusiasm for life – and each other – the Yorks bring colour and vivacity to any occasion they attend left

♔ Sarah won her helicopter wings – the first Royal lady to do so – and Andrew's undying admiration as he pinned them on below, after she completed her training in just 41 flying hours, almost half the time it took him to do so full-time in the Navy

there wondering what I'm going to put on the next day.'

Even so, Sarah found it hard to stop melancholy creeping in sometimes. 'When Andrew is away, I can't wait to see him – it's lonely being a Navy wife,' she said.

There was an unforeseen problem too. 'Andrew comes home on Friday absolutely tired out,' Sarah reported to a friend. 'On Saturday we have a row. On Sunday we make it up but by then he has got to go back to base again.'

'Behind every man there's a good woman?' she queried ironically around this time. 'I mean an *exhausted* one!' she added.

Tim Graham

Hulton Picture Company

👑 *All of an age, Diana, Sarah and Andrew* below *enjoy the sporting life. Sarah's inclusion in the Royal Family has meant that the more decorous Princess of Wales now has a contemporary and confidante in her sister-in-law. Together, they have been known to get up to japes on the fashionable ski-slopes of Klosters*

Andrew missed Sarah as desperately as she missed him. It was hard to look on Buckingham Palace as a marital home, though she tried not to pine while he was away. They were in the process of having a house built for them at Sunninghill Park, but while they waited, they wanted to have something more convenient for Andrew's job. After an initial unhappy choice, they were offered the use of King Hussein of Jordan's Castlewood House on the fringes of Windsor Great Park.

Their dream house was slow in taking shape. Sunninghill Park is about five miles from Windsor Castle, next to Ascot racecourse and set in five acres of grounds. Many people have criticized the design of this private residence, but it is very much in keeping with the personalities of the Yorks: though large, it is quite simple, and potentially very comfortable. Sarah is in sole charge of the interior decorating. 'Sarah's the family manager holding the purse-strings,' Andrew has said, quite happy with the situation.

Learning to fly

Shortly after getting married, Sarah decided to learn to fly for Andrew's sake. 'Flying is his life and I want to be part of his life,' she said. It also made her feel nearer to him when he was away.

Three afternoons a week she left the Palace and her busy schedule to spend some hours being taught by Colin Beckwith in a Piper Warrior. She was so happily voluble during these lessons that she was given the code name 'Chatterbox 1' by the air-traffic controllers. After just 22 hours of teaching, she made her first solo flight and was presented with her wings early in 1987.

'I am certainly surprised by her, she does everything very well indeed,' said Andrew. And hardly had she flown her first loop the loop (yelling 'I've done it!') than she signed up for helicopter lessons as well.

This time it took 41 hours of flying for Sarah to gain her wings in a Jet Ranger helicopter. As soon as she had got them, she took

Tim Graham

'Flying is his life and I want to be part of his life'

SARAH

👑 *Uninhibited by Royal reserve, the Yorks share an undisguised and spontaneous camaraderie that makes them excellent ambassadors to the newer nations. The guests at a banquet in Edmonton loved it when the Duchess reacted to some cheeky remarks made by her husband by grabbing him by the throat and pretending to strangle him* right

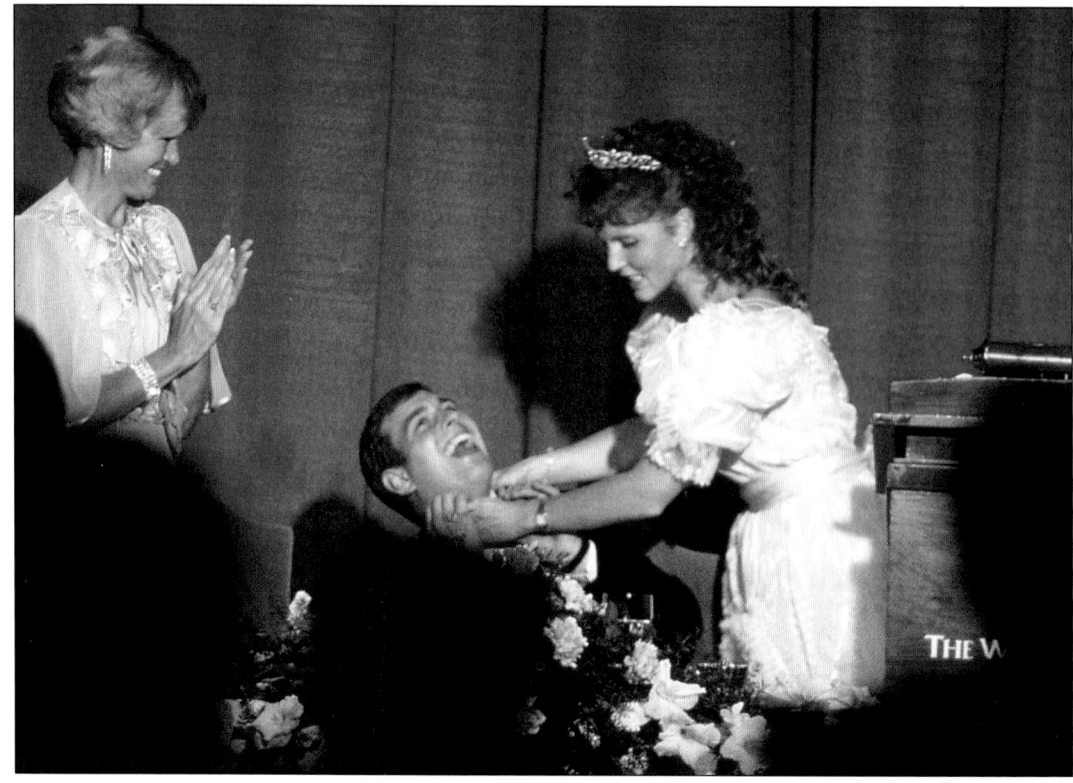

Tim Graham

Andrew on a flight. 'He didn't need a sick bag,' she reported proudly. 'She never ceases to amaze me,' Andrew muttered later.

Apart from Andrew's absences, Sarah was clearly enjoying married life. She continued to live up to her boast that she was a hard-working girl. 'The more you do the more you can do, and I love being a wife, I love my official duties and I love publishing . . . and I love flying too. So I'll just keep on doing as much as I can. Keeps you young.'

Adjusting to Royal etiquette

A chance for a second honeymoon came quite quickly when the Yorks joined the Prince and Princess of Wales at Klosters in Switzerland for a week-long skiing break. Diana and Sarah staged a cabaret on ice where they pretended to have a fight, until Prince Charles became annoyed. On another occasion, Sarah and Diana vigorously relived their childhood with a pillow fight in their chalet at Wolfgang.

It wasn't just Charles's disapproval that was incurred back in Britain, at Sarah's first Royal Ascot. Sarah and Diana were snapped as they used their umbrellas to prod their friend Lulu Blacker in the bottom. Was Sarah going to be a bad influence on Diana? the newspapers asked.

These comments wounded Sarah, which was probably why she lost her temper with Andrew during a public engagement later in 1987. Andrew had publicly corrected her on some matter of royal etiquette, and she flew out at him loudly. 'Why do you keep embarrassing me and pointing it out in front of other people when I get things wrong? It's not very charitable. Why don't you wait until we are on our own? Unlike some people I haven't been doing this for 27 years. I'm going to make mistakes and get things wrong. You might as well accept this and just help me.' But Sarah's temper is sharp and short-lived. As soon as she had had her say, she pinched Andrew's cheeks and kissed him.

On another occasion she said, 'Every day I try to learn something because I've got so much to do. I'm really a newcomer and I try very hard to learn the right way, and to do what is best for them, for the Family.'

Tour of Canada

The Yorks' first major foreign visit was a 25-day tour of Canada in July 1987.

The Canadian press was unkind to the Royal couple, calling her 'Big Red' and 'Rowdy Fergie', and Andrew the 'Duke of Pork', a label that was later modified to describe Sarah also. But the tour was a success, and the people loved them. 'It's Sarah they want to see, not me,' Andrew said, delightedly.

Their first wedding anniversary occurred

Hulton Picture Company

while they were away. They were presented with fur coats of grey beaver and light brown fox. Sarah politely donned hers immediately, sparking off protests from animal rights groups around the world.

Canoeing and camping

At the end of the official 12-day tour, they rounded off the trip with a holiday. Their holiday was not a rest. They planned a 300-mile epic journey down the Hanbury and Thelon rivers. Sarah left her dresses behind and wore army fatigues, with a Davy Crocket racoon headband and a large Bowie knife in her belt.

For ten days they paddled their canoe hundreds of miles from civilization, camping out at night on the river banks. Andrew stuck a sign on their canoe which read, 'Never underestimate the power of this woman.'

👑 *Being a new Royal is not all play and no work: the Duchess of York takes a special personal interest in charity work. She brings her own unique sense of style and warmth to the causes she champions and is only too ready to get down to meeting those less privileged than she* above

👑 *To Bea or not to Bea: the little Princess takes charge of an unexpected present* below *as she is introduced to an adoring audience by her fond parents. The birth of Princess Beatrice in 1988 has added to the York family's happiness but has in no way kept them from their busy working lives*

Tim Graham

Early 1988 found them abroad again, this time in Hollywood, and it was abundantly plain that they were still supremely happy with their marriage. 'About 18 months ago I made what is probably the greatest and best decision of my life,' Andrew announced one evening at a celebrity dinner. 'I married the woman at the end of the table.'

Starting a family

Later in his speech he made an even more interesting announcement. 'She is also expecting in August although some people may not have noticed,' he said.

In a speech of her own, Sarah alluded to her pregnancy in passing, too: 'So we decided – that is, all three of us – this person in here too . . .' she said, patting her stomach.

While she was pregnant, Sarah saw no reason not to go skiing as usual with the Royal party at Klosters. The press, like a bevy of disapproving nannies, told her in print that she was selfishly endangering her unborn child. Sarah was understandably annoyed. 'I'm 100 per cent fit and I always moderate my skiing to suit the conditions,' she said.

Tragedy on the slopes

But it was during this skiing trip that the Royal party went off piste and Major Hugh Lindsay was killed in an avalanche. Sarah was not with them when the accident happened. 'Klosters was a nightmare. I wish I had taken the advice to stay at home. I can't believe I was lucky enough not to be skiing that afternoon,' she told a friend sadly.

Hulton Picture Company

John Shelley

♛ *Always one for the active life, Sarah enjoys riding, an activity she often shares with the Queen. Combining this interest with her increasing participation in charity work, she rode the thoroughbred racer Aldaniti along the Long Drive at Windsor in March 1987 in aid of a cancer fund* above

♛ *Seldom have Royals been seen in such work gear, but the new Yorks donned this special clothing when visiting the Yellow Knife Giant Mines on their tour of Canada in 1987* left. *Sarah has had a strong influence on her husband in loosening up the conventionally stuffy Royal image*

Pregnancy was not something that Sarah enjoyed. 'I can't wait to get the whole thing over with,' she said. It became worse when she put on a lot of weight. Her taste for boiled eggs, toast 'soldiers' and mayonnaise did not help the problem either.

William Hill the bookmakers began to give short odds on her giving birth to twins. And during the later stages of her pregnancy, when presenting a rosette for a winning breed of Shire horse, she said, 'Who gets the rosette – me or the horse? I'm beginning to feel like a horse.'

A baby princess

Her family were in no doubt that she would enjoy motherhood once she gave birth. 'Sarah is very good with children,' her sister Jane said, 'but somehow we've never talked about how many she'd like.'

What made those last few weeks even worse was that Andrew was unable to be with her. Luckily he arrived back in time to drive her to the hospital.

SETTLING DOWN

Their first child, a daughter, Princess Beatrice, was born on 18 August 1988. Sarah's labour was induced, and towards the end of it she was given an epidural to ease the pain. Andrew stayed by her side throughout. 'She had a tough time but she came through very well,' he said with some relief after the birth. He told the well-wishers who clustered around the hospital waiting for news of the infant, 'My daughter is gorgeous, but I'm biased. She is very pretty. It feels wonderful to be a father.'

Unpopular with the press

Six weeks after the birth, Sarah left Princess Beatrice ('baby beetroot') with her nanny and flew off for a tour of Australia. Comparisons were drawn with Diana, who took William on tour with her when he was some months older than Beatrice, but nobody seemed to notice that Diana had never done such a thing again: a royal tour was too gruelling for a baby.

Nevertheless, this act dented Sarah's popularity considerably with the general public, partly because leaving children, considered so ordinary in the past, was thoroughly out of fashion in the 1970s and 80s. What made it

Tim Graham

BUDGIE SAVES THE DAY

Tim Graham

In the days of her engagement, Sarah was asked whether she had ever thought of writing a book herself. 'Yes,' she said, 'but I haven't totally and utterly taken it out of the computer between my ears . . . I do have very specific ideas but I'm afraid I'm not going to let you know. I don't mean to be rude.'

It was when she was first pregnant that she got her ideas down on paper: two children's books about a helicopter called Budgie. The deals for the books were handled by a US agent whose clients include Joan Collins and Shirley Conran. Predictably, British feathers were ruffled by this, but even more so when Sarah went on the publicity tour for the books *right*. She plugged them on radio and television, and the American serial rights alone went for £77,000.

The greatest fuss was made by the fact that it appeared that Sarah would be keeping 90 per cent of the money the books would earn, giving only 10 per cent to charity

'*She sparkles,*

radiating warmth

and a sense of

fun . . .

she's a real

woman'

ANDREW ON SARAH

👑 *After the initial fashion* faux *pas of the all too conspicuous dressing she displayed on public occasions, the Duchess of York has acquired a surer and subtler touch. She still makes spectacular appearances* left, *but they are now greeted with gasps of admiration*

worse was when Sarah elected to extend her stay for some time *à deux* with Andrew and for another week with her sister and mother on the Badarra island on the Great Barrier Reef. This was considered the last straw, and even Andrew was moved to defend his wife.

'If they bothered to think about it for one second, Beatrice is much better off at home where things are stable,' he said.

Since their marriage, Sarah has had to struggle hard for general popularity. The press pick on her constantly, on the watch for gaffes or criticizing her appearance. They love to make out that she is a bad mother, though – in common with many women who are still very much in love with their husbands – she looks after her two children very well but believes they come second.

Popular within the Family

She has no such popularity problems within the Royal Family, where she continues to be liked by them all.

The Queen, particularly, has a soft spot for her; they have tea and dinner together quite frequently. They enjoy talking about country matters, being a naval wife (as the Queen was too) and their shared love of animals. Sarah and the Queen also regularly ride together after breakfast on the Royal estates at Sandringham, Windsor and Balmoral. The Queen has been known to refer to her as 'my daughter'.

Sarah keeps her head down and hopes that her present unpopularity will pass – as it passed for Princess Anne, Princess Margaret and Princess Michael of Kent before her. She keeps very busy, despite having to give up her career.

A working patron

An example of how she operates is her work with the Search 88 Cancer Trust. Gareth Pyne-James, the founder, had the idea of producing a book of photographs of Britain taken on a selected day by ordinary members of the public, the proceeds of which would go to the Trust. Sarah was able to offer her practical experience of publishing along with her enthusiasm for the cause, making it clear that she was not going to be a mere figurehead.

Using Diana as her role model, she selects organizations in which she is genuinely interested and then works behind the scenes to see how they operate before undertaking public functions on their behalf. Her patronages include charities ranging from drug dependency and care of the lonely to the Tate Gallery Foundation.

And, slowly, Sarah has been paying attention to what the press say about her. Her wardrobe has smartened considerably and she has kept her weight down, even during her second pregnancy, when she looked in good shape right to the end.

'He is my support, my main right arm'

SARAH ON ANDREW

👑 *Princess Eugenie Victoria Helena makes her first public appearance* below *after her birth on 23 March 1990. She was christened, like her elder sister, with names that hark back to a more opulent and indulgent past, confirming the popular opinion of the Yorks as the most romantic of the Royals*

Their second daughter was born at 7.58 pm on Friday 23 March 1990. The new Princess, who was given the names Eugenie Victoria Helena even before she left hospital, weighed 7lb 1½oz and was delivered by Caesarean section because she was lying in the breach position. Prince Andrew made a last-minute dash from his naval base at Devonport to be at Sarah's side when she gave birth.

Love and kisses

'He is my support, my main right arm,' Sarah has said of her husband, and their very romantic love for each other is still apparent after two children. 'Andrew is like a teddy bear – cuddly,' Sarah has said, and the relationship remains very physical on a playful as well as a sensual level.

'Sarah is vivacious, cheerful, outgoing, vibrant. She sparkles, radiating warmth and a sense of fun,' Prince Andrew has said fondly of his wife. He can still hardly believe his luck that he chose so well. 'She's a very open girl. She loves to make people feel happy.'

But perhaps the secret of Andrew's enduring passion for Sarah is summed up in one simple comment he has made about her: 'She's a real woman.'

Tim Graham